Apples Everywhere

Debora Pearson

"I've got some more apples, Dad!" called Kim as she carried the basket filled with apples over to the tractor.

At the Chan family farm in the Wenatchee Valley where Kim lived, it was apple-picking time. Thousands of apples were in the orchard. Some of them were still on the trees waiting to be harvested. Other apples had been picked and were ready to be sold. They sat in baskets waiting to go to market.

Welcome
to the
Wenatchee
Valley

3

Kim handed her father her basket and watched as he loaded it into the trailer.

"We've picked a lot of apples so far," she said as she turned to go back to the orchard.

"We sure have," agreed Kim's dad. He leaned against the trailer and wiped his forehead. "Soon these apples will be taking a trip. They'll leave our farm here in Washington and they'll be sent to places far away. Our apples will go everywhere—all over America."

Kim's sister, Kate, handed another full basket to their father.

"Some of these apples will be baked in pies or made into applesauce," Kate said.

"And some of them will be eaten, like this!" said Kim biting into the big, shiny apple in her hand. She chewed and swallowed. Then she patted her stomach and grinned.

"Our apples do go everywhere!" Kim laughed, taking another bite.

After the apples had been harvested, some of the apples from Kim's farm were loaded into boxes onto Mr. Carr's 18-wheel truck. Mr. Carr was taking his truck full of fruits and vegetables to the Alaskan community of Tok.

Mr. Carr knew that people in Tok were waiting to buy fruits and vegetables from his truck because they were so fresh—especially his apples.

It was a long drive along the Alaska Highway. Sometimes Mr. Carr would spot a caribou looking at the truck as it went by.

When Mr. Carr arrived in Tok, he parked his truck near the Visitor Center. Before he could sell his food, he had to turn his truck into a store.

He opened the back door on the truck's trailer and pushed some stairs up to the door. He set up his sign where people could see it.

"I'm almost ready," he said to himself.

Adam and his friend, Sam, ran up the stairs as soon as Mr. Carr put the "Open" sign on the door.

"Do you have potatoes, tomatoes, and apples today?" Adam asked as he came through the door. "My dad wants to make stew and an apple pie tonight."

"I need apples, too," said Sam. "I'm going to make baked apples with my sister. She said she would show me how."

"Step right this way!" said Mr. Carr as he opened some boxes. "I've got potatoes here, tomatoes there, and lots of apples everywhere," he sang out, pointing to the fruits and vegetables on display.

A draft of icy air shot through the truck as the door opened again.

"Hi, Adam," said Deepa, shutting the door behind her. She looked around her. "Wow! I've never seen a store like this one before!"

"Deepa just moved here from Detroit," Adam told Sam and Mr. Carr. "Her mom teaches at our school."

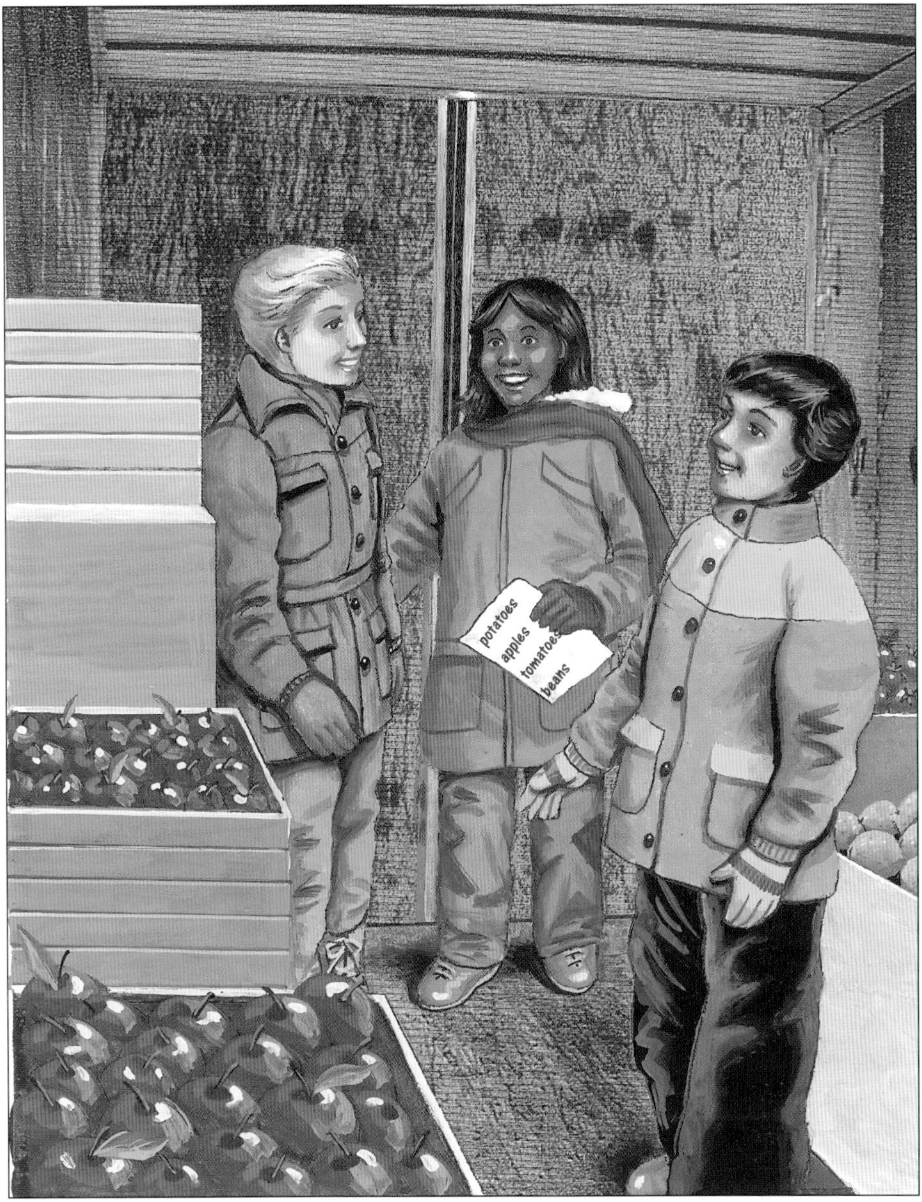
potatoes
apples
tomatoes
beans

"It must be really different living here now," Sam said. "Do you miss living in Detroit?"

"Well," said Deepa, thinking, "I miss some things, like going to all the different shops with my mom. But some things are the same, too, like going skating at the arena and going to the library to take out books. Then there are some things that are really different, like watching the northern lights. I saw them last night for the first time. It was amazing to watch the beautiful colors lighting up the sky."

"The northern lights are beautiful, all right," said Sam. "Hey," he added, "I'm going to the library later this afternoon. Maybe I'll see you there. Right now, though, I'd better get these apples home."

"I'm supposed to buy apples, too," said Deepa, checking her list. "My mom wants to make apple chutney."

"Chutney? What's that?" asked Adam.

"Chutney is made of fruit cooked with ginger and spices," Deepa explained. "People in India serve it with their food."

Deepa smiled and added, "But you don't have to be from India to eat chutney—people everywhere like it."

"I'd like to try apple chutney," said Sam. "I wonder if it would be hard to make."

"No," said Deepa. "You have to chop up the apples, though. My mom likes to make it because it reminds her of where she grew up. In her hometown of Chennai in India, she bought apples and spices at the market. She went to the market every week with her mother when she was young."

"Apples in India," said Adam.

"Apples in Tok," laughed Deepa.

They heard a "crunch" from Sam as he took an apple from his bag and bit into it. He chewed and swallowed. Then he patted his stomach and grinned.

"Mmmmm!" said Sam. "Apples, apples, everywhere!"

Questions

1. What are all the place names mentioned in the book?

2. Why do you think Mr. Carr's truck of fruits and vegetables was welcome in Tok?

3. What are some of the differences between shopping in the market in India and shopping in the place where Sam, Adam, and Deepa bought their apples?

4. How is shopping for food in your community the same as shopping for food in Sam's community? How is it different?